SUPER SIMPLE

AFTER SCHOOL ACTIVITIES

By Cara Copperman

Illustrated by Leo Abbett

LOWELL HOUSE JUVENILE

LOS ANGELES

NTC/Contemporary Publishing Group

NOTE TO THE READER:

The craft supplies used in this book are available at any arts and crafts store unless otherwise indicated. When doing the activities in this book, always have the following items on hand: measuring cup, measuring spoons, wooden or metal spoons, ruler, and scissors. These are not listed under What You'll Need unless they serve a special purpose.

Published by Lowell House
A division of NTC/Contemporary Publishing Group, Inc.
4255 West Touhy Avenue, Lincolnwood (Chicago), Illinois 60712 U.S.A.

Managing Director and Publisher: Jack Artenstein
Director of Publishing Services: Rena Copperman
Editorial Director: Brenda Pope-Ostrow
Project Editor: Dianne J. Woo
Typesetter: Carolyn Wendt
Cover Designer: Treesha Runnells Vaux

Lowell House books can be purchased at special discounts
when ordered in bulk for premiums and special sales.
Contact Customer Service at the address above,
or call 1-800-323-4900.

Printed and bound in the United States of America

Library of Congress Catalog Card Number: 00-130071

ISBN: 0-7373-0485-5

ML 10 9 8 7 6 5 4 3 2 1

CONTENTS

GLITTER GLOBE

Glitter creates a magical effect when you shake this dome.

WHAT YOU'LL NEED

• empty baby food jar with lid • rubber cement
• small plastic figure (such as a snowman, ornament, or palm tree)
• 1 or 2 tablespoons glitter • glycerin (optional, available at drugstores) • paper towels

DIRECTIONS

❶ Wash and dry the baby food jar and lid thoroughly.

❷ Turn the lid over and put several dabs of rubber cement on the center of the inside as shown. Stand the plastic figure on the cement and let dry.

❸ Fill the jar three-quarters full with water. Add the glitter and, if you wish, several drops of glycerin. Glycerin will thicken the water and cause the glitter to swirl around longer.

❹ Coat the inside rim of the jar with rubber cement. Screw the lid onto the jar. Use the paper towel to wipe off any extra cement that oozes out.

❺ When the glue is dry, shake, shake, shake, and watch the glitter swirl.

4

CATERPILLAR COURSE

Wiggle your way through this obstacle course just like a caterpillar crawling underground. This game is also perfect for a sleepover.

WHAT YOU'LL NEED

• three or more people • pillows, blankets, and things to crawl under or over • one sleeping bag for each person • stopwatch or watch with a second hand (optional)

DIRECTIONS

❶ Select a room in the house that has no sharp or breakable objects.

❷ Create an obstacle course by making a winding path in the room. Make the path go under tables and around chairs and other large obstacles. Put pillows and blankets in the way so that you will have to crawl over and under them.

❸ When the course is ready, have each person get into a sleeping bag and zip it up. Each person goes through the course, one at a time.

❹ To turn the activity into a race, time each person and compare scores. The person to complete the course in the least amount of time wins!

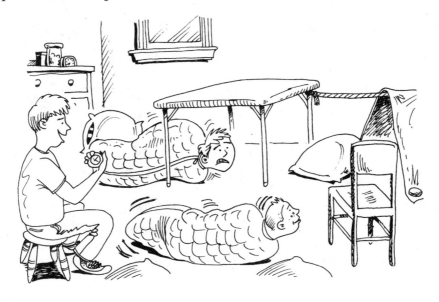

3

TRULY
TROPICAL MEAL

Winter blues got you down? Here's a meal that's sure to make you feel like you're on summer vacation. Turn your dining room into a Hawaiian paradise with these easy, no-cook recipes that serve four.

DESERT ISLAND APPETIZERS

WHAT YOU'LL NEED
• one can sliced pineapple rings • four small plates • ice-cream scooper
• 16 ounces cottage cheese • four stalks celery with leafy tops attached

DIRECTIONS

❶ Ask a grownup to open the can of pineapple.

❷ Lay a pineapple ring in the center of each plate. Place a scoop of cottage cheese in the center of each ring.

❸ Wash and dry the celery, then insert one stalk in the middle of each cottage cheese island so that it looks like a palm tree.

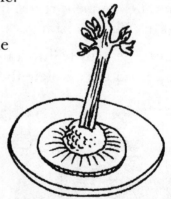

❹ Put the plates in the fridge until you are ready to serve them.

HAWAIIAN CHICKEN BOATS

WHAT YOU'LL NEED
• head of iceberg lettuce • paper towels
• four microwave-safe plates • 1 to 2 pounds diced cooked chicken
• duck sauce (available in the Asian foods section of the supermarket)

DIRECTIONS

❶ Peel the leaves off the head of lettuce, being careful not to tear them. You'll probably need about 16 leaves. Wash them carefully and dry with paper towels.

❷ Place four leaves on each plate, one inside the other, so that they form a cup. Divide the chicken evenly into each of the lettuce cups.

❸ Spoon duck sauce over the chicken, or put the sauce in a bowl on the table so that people can use as much as they like.

❹ Keep the plates in the fridge until ready to serve. You can serve this dish warm or cold. To serve warm, put each plate into the microwave for 1 minute on high right before serving.

SWEET SURFIN' STRAWBERRIES

WHAT YOU'LL NEED

• rubber spatula • four plates • one tub whipped cream • butter knife
• four bananas • 1 pint strawberries (washed and dried) or whole frozen strawberries

DIRECTIONS

❶ Using the spatula, cover each plate with a thin layer of whipped cream. This will be the "water" for your Surfin' Strawberries.

❷ Slice each banana in half lengthwise to create two long "surfboards."

❸ Place two banana surfboards on each plate on top of the water.

❹ Place one "surfer" strawberry on each surfboard, then place more strawberries on top of the whipped cream to suggest swimmers in the water.

4 MARBLE
MEMO MINDERS

You won't forget where you put your papers if you stick 'em up where you can see 'em.

WHAT YOU'LL NEED

• paper towels • liquid starch • 9-by-13-inch baking dish • three clean tablespoons
• acrylic paints • paper cup • distilled water • eyedropper
• Popsicle sticks or disposable comb • several sheets white construction paper
• rolling pin • sheet of thick cardboard • glue • magnets

DIRECTIONS

❶ Spread out some of the paper towels over your workspace. Pour 1½ inches liquid starch into the baking dish. Lay a paper towel gently on top of the starch as shown, then pick it up slowly. This should remove any air bubbles from the surface of the starch.

❷ Using one of the clean tablespoons, put 2 tablespoons acrylic paint into the paper cup. Using another clean tablespoon, add 2 tablespoons distilled water to the paper cup. Mix using the third clean tablespoon. Drop 5 drops of the paint mixture onto the starch in the baking dish.

❸ Using a Popsicle stick, swirl designs in the mixture. This is your marble design.

❹ Now it's time to transfer your marble design to paper. Lay a sheet of construction paper on top of the mixture, letting the middle of the paper touch first as shown. Gently smooth down the edges.

❺ Wait 15 seconds, then lift the paper carefully. Lay it on the paper towels, paint side up. Lay another paper towel on top of the paper. Roll the rolling pin twice over the paper and paper towels as shown to remove any excess paint. Pull the top paper towel off, then repeat with another clean paper towel. Set your design aside to dry.

❻ Use the cardboard to skim the surface of the liquid in the baking dish so that you can create a different design. Add more drops of paint mixture if you wish, and repeat steps 3 through 5.

❼ When your designs are dry, cut them into shapes. Glue the shapes to the magnets and stick them on your fridge or locker. Create different designs using a variety of colors.

HERE'S

···

THE STORY...

Whether it's happy, sad, dramatic, or funny, everyone has a story to tell. The story of your own life is called an autobiography. Get yours down on paper and you'll have a record of it forever.

WHAT YOU'LL NEED
• pencils and scrap paper • family photos • old magazines
• colored pens, pencils, and markers • high-quality colored paper or construction paper
• two pieces colored cardboard • hole puncher • string or ribbon

DIRECTIONS

❶ Begin by writing the text. Write on scrap paper so that you can cross things out and move things around. Start with the basics: your name, birthday, hometown, vital stats (height, weight, eye color, whether you're a boy or girl). You can start from when you were born and write about what your life was like growing up, or you can start more recently and tell your life in the form of a story.

❷ Select photos, make drawings, and cut out clippings from magazines to illustrate events or other things in your story. Get a parent's permission to use any family photos.

❸ Now, do the layout for your autobiography. Use scrap paper again to plan out where the text will flow and where the pictures will go. When you're ready, copy the text onto the high-quality paper. You can do this in pen or on the computer. Then paste in your pictures.

❹ Design a front and back cover for your book using markers and the colored cardboard. Title it "My Story," or think of something clever.

❺ Punch five holes along either the top or the left side of the book. You may need to punch a few pages at a time. Bind your book by tying string or ribbon through the holes.

6

G O N E

F I S H I N '

If you and your friends are fishing for something to do on a sunny afternoon, try this game.

WHAT YOU'LL NEED

• **3 to 10 people** • **string** • **yardsticks and/or empty wrapping paper tubes,
one for each person** • **masking tape** • **small horseshoe magnets, one for each person**
• **foam trays, such as meat trays, sushi trays, or takeout-food trays** • **crayons or
non-water-based markers** • **large metal paper clips** • **plastic or inflatable kiddie pool**

DIRECTIONS

❶ To make the fishing poles, cut 2 to 3 feet of string for each pole. Use masking tape to attach the strings to the yardsticks and/or paper tubes. Tie a magnet onto the other end with string as shown.

❷ Cut fish shapes out of the foam trays. Color and decorate the fish with the crayons or markers. Fasten a paper clip onto the mouth area of each fish.

❸ Now you're ready to play! First, fill the kiddie pool with water.

❹ When the pool is full, everyone stands or sits around the pool and tries to catch the fish using a magnetized fishing pole. The person with the most fish wins!

Something Extra

If it's raining, or if you don't want to play outside, this game can be played indoors. Make the fish out of cardboard or paper, or cut out pictures of fish from magazines. Attach the paper clips and scatter the fish on the floor. Have everyone sit on her or his own "pillow boat" in a circle and start reeling them in!

7

2 0
QUESTIONS

This is a classic game you and a friend or family member can play anywhere—in a car, on the bus, over the phone, even by E-mail.

WHAT YOU'LL NEED
• a friend or family member

DIRECTIONS

1 Pick an object. Don't tell the other person what it is or anything about it.

2 The other person asks you 20 "yes or no" questions, one at a time, to try to figure out what the object is. Sample questions include "Is it an animal?" and "Can it be eaten?" If a question cannot be answered with yes or no, the question must be reworded and asked again.

3 The other person can make guesses before the 20 questions have been asked, but each guess counts as a question. If the person guesses correctly before the 20 questions have been used, he or she wins. If the person does not figure out the answer before the 20 questions have been asked, you win.

4 Now switch places and have the other person pick an object.

8 BUBBLE-BLOWING FUN

Forget those cheap plastic bubble wands you buy at the store. Make massive bubbles in your own backyard with things around the house!

WHAT YOU'LL NEED

• ¼ cup dishwashing liquid • 1 tablespoon baby shampoo • bucket or large, shallow dish
• wire hanger • towel or glove • duct tape • two straws
• piece of string three to four times the length of one straw • funnel

DIRECTIONS

To create the soap solution, mix together the dishwashing liquid, baby shampoo, and 2 cups water in the bucket. You may want to add more or less of each of these ingredients as you experiment with your bubbles. Now you're going to make three different wands.

To make wand #1:

❶ Cover your dominant hand (the one you write with) with the towel or glove for protection. Hold the wire hanger in the other hand. Bend the hook part of the hanger down to its base to form a loop as shown. Wrap the end and base with duct tape. This is your wand handle.

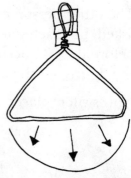

❷ Bend the rest of the hanger into a circular or oblong shape as shown. This is your wand. Dip it into the soap solution, then wave it in one direction and watch the bubble form. You can also hold the wand up in the air and run or walk with it, watching the bubbles trail behind you. Experiment by twisting the wand into different shapes.

To make wand #2:

Thread the string through both straws, then tie the ends together in a knot. Tie another knot about 2 inches from the first knot as shown. This is your wand handle. Dip the wand into the solution and wave it in the air or run with it to make cool-shaped bubbles.

To make wand #3:

Dip the large end of the funnel into the soap solution and blow lightly through the small end. Be careful not to swallow any of the solution. Experiment by moving the funnel up, down, right, left, and in circles as you blow to close the bubbles and create long trails.

KNOCK YOUR
SOCKS OFF

Here's a game that requires just a couple of materials, but lots of skill.

WHAT YOU'LL NEED

• **three or more people** • **two socks from each player** • **blanket or bedsheet**

DIRECTIONS

❶ Roll each sock into a ball or tie it into a knot.

❷ Spread the blanket on the floor and put the socks in the center.

❸ Each player grabs an edge of the blanket and waves it up and down. The object is to bounce everyone else's socks off. The winner is the last person who has a sock on the blanket.

WHAT'S IN STORE?

Are you and your friends sitting around with nothing to do? Pull out a deck of cards and play this fun, fast-thinking game.

WHAT YOU'LL NEED
• **five to eight friends** • **deck of cards**

DIRECTIONS

❶ Everyone sits around a table. Each player picks a type of store she or he wants to be (a grocery store, a clothing store, a baby-supply store, a toy store, a hardware store, etc.). No two people can choose the same store. All the players must memorize who is what store.

❷ Pick one person to be the dealer. The dealer shuffles the deck and deals one card to each person, face up, starting with the person on the right. The dealer keeps dealing until two people have the same card face up in front of them. Then the dealer stops dealing.

❸ The two people with the same card immediately stand up and call out the name of something in the other person's store. Whoever calls out something first gets a point, as long as it hasn't been said already and as long as it can be found in the other person's store. If the person calls out an incorrect item, she loses a point.

❹ The dealer continues handing out cards until the entire deck has been dealt. The player with the most points wins.

❺ If more than eight people are playing, you may want to use two decks of cards.

HAMMER!

PLEASE
MR. POSTMAN

Postcards are an easy way to get your personalized message across, and you don't even need to be on vacation to send one.

WHAT YOU'LL NEED

• photo • 4-by-6-inch index card • glue • colored markers or highlighting pens
• white paper (optional) • self-adhesive clear laminate • postage stamp (optional)

DIRECTIONS

❶ Pick a photo you like and make a photocopy of it.

❷ Trim the photocopy so that it's 4 by 6 inches, the same size as the index card. Glue the photocopy to the lined side of the index card and let dry.

❸ Now color the photo with markers or highlighting pens. If you like, write a caption, speech bubble, or thought bubble on white paper, then cut it out and glue it onto the photo.

❹ Cover the image with the laminate as shown and trim off any ragged edges. You've just made a postcard!

❺ On the back of the postcard, draw a line down the center. Write a message for a special someone on the left-hand side as shown. Write the person's address on the right-hand side.

❻ Stick on a postage stamp and mail your card, place it on that special someone's door or locker, or slip it into the person's notebook or bag.

GOOD LUCK GARLAND

Who doesn't need good luck every now and then? Well, this garland isn't guaranteed to bring you luck, but it sure makes a great decoration.

WHAT YOU'LL NEED
• two sheets white construction paper • pencil
• three colors of construction paper, two sheets each color • hole puncher • 2 yards twine

DIRECTIONS

1 Think of three objects that represent you or what you like: a baseball, a car, a flower, a guitar, a smiley face, or any item that's simple and easy to cut out.

2 Draw each of the objects on the white paper. Make the first object 2 to 3 inches long, the second 4 inches long, and the third 5 inches long. Be sure to leave space at the top of each to punch a hole.

3 Cut out each object. These will be your templates.

4 Choose one color construction paper for each object. Cut out 12 of each shape, using the templates as a guide. Fold or stack the construction paper so that you can cut out more than one shape at a time.

5 Punch a hole in the top of each cutout.

6 Fold the twine in half, leaving enough at each end to tie a 1½-inch loop. String one of each item onto the twine. Tie a knot after the last item as shown. Then add another set of three items. Tie a knot between each set.

7 When you have strung all of the cutouts onto the twine, knot the end and hang the garland over your doorway or your desk.

WRITING
SEEDS

Every writer gets writer's block from time to time. Here's a fun way to get un-blocked.

WHAT YOU'LL NEED
• **AM radio** • **pen or pencil** • **notebook or legal pad** • **egg timer**

DIRECTIONS

❶ Sit at a table or on your bed with the radio next to you. Turn on the radio and move the selector to the bottom of the dial.

❷ Turn the selector knob slowly until you hear someone speaking or singing clearly. It could be a commercial, a conversation, or a song. Take your hand off the knob, set the timer for 15 seconds, and write down as many key words as you can. What you write will become the seed of an idea.

❸ When the timer goes off, stop writing and turn the page. Move the selector to another station and record another 15-second seed. Keep doing this until you have reached the end of the dial.

❹ Review all your seeds. Select one that looks interesting and start writing. Don't stop to think; just write whatever comes into your head. Who knows? Your seed may sprout into a story!

Something Extra

If you don't get good reception on your radio, use the TV instead. Use the remote control to go from channel to channel. Include cable or satellite channels if you wish. Don't look at the screen; focus on your notebook and write down what you hear.

POCKET
TROLL

This little pal is small enough to fit inside your pocket or hang on a keychain. It may even bring you a little luck.

WHAT YOU'LL NEED

• **two bottle corks** • **white glue** • **two googly eyes** • **six mini pom-poms**
• **crepe paper** • **cloth or felt** • **black permanent marker**

DIRECTIONS

❶ Glue one cork on top of the other cork. About ½ inch down from the top edge of the top cork, glue on the googly eyes. Just below the eyes, glue on a pom-pom for the nose.

❷ To make a hat, apply glue around the cork just above the eyes. Wrap a strip of crepe paper around the glued area. Twist the paper at the top as shown. Glue a pom-pom at the tip.

❸ Now cut out pieces of cloth or felt using the scissors. Apply glue to the bottom cork and attach the pieces to make the clothing for your troll.

❹ Attach one pom-pom for each hand and one for each foot.

❺ For the finishing touch, draw a mouth on your troll that reflects its mood. Your troll can be happy, sad, surprised, angry…whatever suits it best! Gather more corks and make a treasure trove of trolls.

Something Extra

To make your troll into a keychain, buy a plain keychain at a craft store. Attach it to the back of your troll by pushing it into the cork and securing it with glue.

LITTLE

BOXES

Try your hand at boxing—on paper, that is! This is a great game to play in the car or whenever you and a friend are trying to pass the time.

WHAT YOU'LL NEED
• paper • pens in two different colors • a friend

DIRECTIONS

❶ Make 10 rows of 10 dots each on the paper. The rows of dots should line up as straight as possible.

❷ Each person selects a pen color. Decide who will go first.

❸ The first person makes a line by connecting two dots either across or down (not diagonally) with the pen. The second person does the same with the other pen.

❹ The object is to complete as many boxes as possible and to keep your opponent from completing boxes. When you complete a box, write your initial inside and take another turn.

❺ When all of the dots are connected, every finished box should have an initial in it. The person with the most boxes wins!

E Z KITE

Kite making has never been easier than this, and you can do it with things you probably have around the house.

WHAT YOU'LL NEED

• **plastic grocery bag** • **ball of string** • **stapler**
• **three pieces colored ribbon, 2 feet each**

DIRECTIONS

1 To make the body of your kite, tie the handles of the grocery bag together with the end of the ball of string.

2 Staple one end of each ribbon to the bottom of the bag as shown. These will form the tail of your kite.

3 That's it! Now take your kite out for a test flight. Find an open, windy space outdoors. Start running, holding up the ball of string with the bag trailing behind you. As the bag fills with air, let the string out little by little, and watch your kite fly!

S A N D
A N D   S E A

This creative candy sculpture may remind you of a day at the beach, but only you will know its secret: it's a tasty treat, too!

WHAT YOU'LL NEED

• **50 Pixy Stix in several different colors**
• **clean, empty baby food jar with lid** • **toothpick**

DIRECTIONS

❶ Empty the Pixy Stix one at a time into the jar, alternating colors. Your object is to use different layers to create a seascape—a landscape of the sea. Imagine what the beach looks like at sundown, for example, and use the appropriate colors. It will take about five sticks to fill one layer.

❷ To make a sand hill, place the open end of a Pixy Stick inside the jar and hold it right next to the glass as the candy pours out.

❸ To make a seagull, pour a layer of blue candy to create the sky. Again, it will take about five sticks to fill one layer. Then pour half a stick of a different color to make a small mound next to the glass. Cover the mound with more blue Pixy Stix. Poke the pointed end of a toothpick through the blue candy into the center of the mound as shown. There's your seagull!

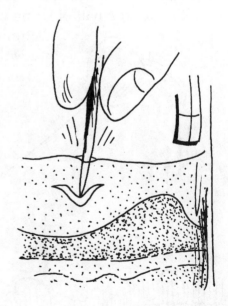

❹ Finish filling the jar with Pixy Stix. It should be completely filled so that the candy won't shift around and ruin your design.

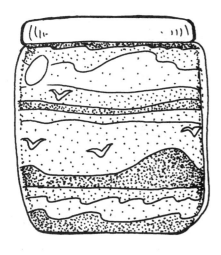

5 Screw the lid on tightly. Place your candy sculpture on your desk to remind you of summertime at the beach.

Something Extra

Once you've created your seascape-in-a-jar, why not try your hand at other designs? See if you can figure out how to create a funny face out of Pixy Stix.

BRAIN

FOOD

Eating a healthy snack after school will keep you energized for the rest of the day. The treats below are great before you start your homework or after you're done. You can make them simple or add your own special touch.

Before you begin, have the following equipment on hand: plates, a fork, spoons, a knife, and your appetite, of course!

CHEESE STIX

WHAT YOU'LL NEED
• nacho cheese sauce or Cheez Whiz • small microwave-safe bowl • pretzel sticks

DIRECTIONS

❶ Pour some cheese sauce into the bowl.

❷ Following the directions on the cheese sauce container, heat the cheese in the microwave.

❸ Dip the pretzel sticks into the sauce and enjoy!

FRUIT BITES

WHAT YOU'LL NEED

• any of the following: grapes, cherries, blueberries, melon,
oranges, peaches, pineapple, raspberries, strawberries, or other fruit
• one of the following dressings: strawberry or lemon yogurt; ½ cup plain yogurt mixed
with peanut butter and honey to taste; cinnamon applesauce • small bowl • toothpicks

DIRECTIONS

❶ Wash the fruit and cut into bite-sized pieces.

❷ Arrange the pieces on a plate.

❸ Mix the dressing in the bowl.

❹ Use a toothpick to spear pieces of the fruit and dip them into the dressing.
For the perfect cool snack on a warm afternoon, try freezing the fruit
before dipping them.

BANANA SANDWICH

WHAT YOU'LL NEED

• two graham crackers • banana • small bowl • honey

DIRECTIONS

❶ Break each graham cracker in half, then arrange the pieces on a plate.

❷ Use a fork to mash the banana in a small bowl. Mix in ¼ teaspoon honey.

❸ Spread the mixture over two of the graham cracker halves.

❹ Place the remaining halves on top to make two sandwiches.

CRUNCHY BITS

WHAT YOU'LL NEED

• banana or apple • peanut butter • granola or cornflakes

DIRECTIONS

❶ Cut the banana or apple into quarters.

❷ Smear peanut butter over each piece of fruit.

❸ Spread the granola or cornflakes on a plate.

❹ Roll the fruit in the granola or cornflakes until coated.

PITCH IN!

Organize a cleanup in your neck of the woods, whether it's a nearby park, the beach, a large, open area, or any place that could use some sprucing up. You and your friends will have fun and help the environment at the same time!

WHAT YOU'LL NEED
• garbage bags • plastic gloves • cookies and juice • a group of friends and volunteers

DIRECTIONS

❶ Pick a date, time, and meeting place for the cleanup, and tell your friends. Remind them to wear old clothes and to wear a watch. Ask a teacher or a few parents to join you and help supervise the cleanup.

❷ On the morning of the cleanup, be the first to get to the meeting place. Once everyone else has arrived, hand each person a garbage bag and a pair of gloves. The gloves will help protect your hands as you scour the area.

❸ Arrange to meet back at the starting point at a certain time. Do not pick up anything that looks sharp or is made of glass or rusted metal. If any object or area looks dangerous, stop working and tell an adult immediately. Make sure everyone understands these directions before you all set out.

❹ Have everyone break up into pairs or small groups and let the cleanup begin! When the cleanup is over, give each other a pat on the back and enjoy a well-deserved snack of cookies and juice.

F I S H   O U T
O F   W A T E R

Is there something fishy here? No, it's just an optical illusion you can create in a snap!

WHAT YOU'LL NEED
• white paper • pencil • tape • colored markers

DIRECTIONS

1 Cut out two small squares of paper, 2 by 2 inches each.

2 On one square, draw the outline of a fishbowl. The outline should fill almost the entire paper. On the other square, draw a small fish in the center.

3 Place the pieces of paper back to back so that the drawings are on the outside. Put the pencil in between the pieces of paper as shown.

4 Tape the pieces of paper together and to the pencil, making sure not to bend the paper.

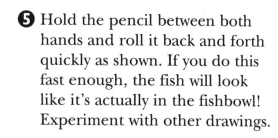

5 Hold the pencil between both hands and roll it back and forth quickly as shown. If you do this fast enough, the fish will look like it's actually in the fishbowl! Experiment with other drawings.

21 FINGERPRINT
FUN

No two people have the same set of fingerprints. Here's your chance to leave your mark with every letter you send!

WHAT YOU'LL NEED
• newspapers • ink pad • unlined paper
• colored pens • paper towels • unlined index cards, any size

DIRECTIONS

❶ This will get messy! Spread the newspapers over your workspace.

❷ Press your index finger (your pointer finger) in the ink, then press it on the unlined paper. Does your fingerprint look too light or too blotchy? Do a few tests until you figure out the right amount of ink and pressure you'll need. Use different fingers, including your thumb, and turn them in different directions.

❸ To make a baby foot, make a fist with one hand. Press your fist, pinky side down, in the ink, then stamp your hand onto the paper. Use your index finger to stamp five toes at the top of your fist print. Once you get the hang of it, invent some shapes of your own. You can add details with colored pens to turn the shapes into animals, people, or objects. Use a wet paper towel to wipe your hands from time to time, and dry them with a dry paper towel.

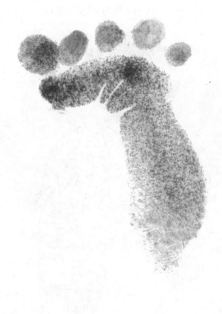

4 Think of a scene that you can put onto a note card. It can be a collection of footprints, a playground scene, a zoo, or two people holding hands.

5 Fold an index card in half. Stamp fingerprints on the front of the card to create your scene, then let them dry. Draw on and around the fingerprints to complete your scene. Write a poem, rhyme, or simple message on the card. Make lots of note cards to have on hand when you want to give a gift to a special someone.

L I A R
L I A R

Studying in a group can turn a tough subject into a fun shared experience. You can also play this game to learn more about your friends.

WHAT YOU'LL NEED
• several friends • index cards, any size • pencils

DIRECTIONS

❶ Have each person write four facts on an index card and letter them A through D. One of the facts must be false. They can be facts about what you're studying, or little-known facts about the person. Have each person write the letter of the false fact on the back of the card. Repeat until there are 20 cards total.

❷ Each person holds up a card, fact side up, and asks the other players to guess which fact is false. A player gets one point for each correct answer.

❸ Whether you're studying for a test or just getting to know each other better, this activity can beef up your knowledge about the subject AND about your friends!

CANDY FLOWERPOT

It's a fact: Candy and flowers make people happy. Make yourself REALLY happy with this candy creation.

WHAT YOU'LL NEED
• newspapers • empty, clean pint-sized ice-cream tub with lid
• acrylic paints • paintbrush • glue • florist foam
• lollipops • hard candies • ribbon

DIRECTIONS

❶ First, spread the newspapers over your workspace. Paint the ice-cream tub and lid and let dry.

❷ Glue the lid to the bottom of the tub. This will be your flowerpot.

❸ Fill the flowerpot with florist foam. Poke the lollipops into the foam. Cover with hard candies. Glue the ribbon around the neck of the planter and tie it in a bow.

❹ When friends compliment you on your delicious-looking arrangement, offer them something from your garden. Don't worry—you can always plant more!

ALIEN
BOOKENDS

If your books keep falling off the shelves, these funny creatures can lend a hand or two (or three...or four)!

WHAT YOU'LL NEED

• two clean, empty half-gallon milk cartons • sand to fill both cartons • glue • aluminum foil • 16 pipe cleaners • four googly eyes • red rubber band

DIRECTIONS

❶ Fill both milk cartons with sand, then glue the tops closed. Cut enough foil to cover each carton, then wrap the foil around each carton.

❷ Poke two pipe cleaners into the top of each carton to make antennae. Apply glue around the holes to keep the pipe cleaners in place.

❸ Poke the rest of the pipe cleaners into the sides of each alien's "body" to give it six arms. After you poke the holes, take the pipe cleaners out, dab glue on the ends, and put them back in.

❹ Glue googly eyes onto each bookend. Cut the rubber band in half and glue on one-half for each mouth. Give each bookend a different expression.

❺ Add construction paper and foil features such as eyebrows, ears, hats, and clothes. Set up the aliens on your shelf as book guardians.

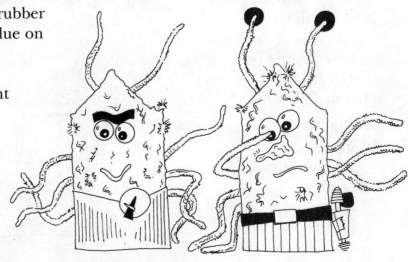

SILLY
....
STORYTELLING

A little nonsense is good for you. Too much nonsense and you have a great story!

WHAT YOU'LL NEED
• **five or more people** • **note cards, five for each person**
• **pens or pencils** • **tape recorder** • **blank tape cassette**

DIRECTIONS

❶ Everyone sits in a circle. Choose a type of story such as science fiction, fairy tale, mystery, romance, or sports. Have each person write down five words that might be used in such a story, one word per card.

❷ Collect the cards and shuffle them. Deal five cards to each person, face down.

❸ Put the blank tape into the tape recorder and give it to the first person. Have him flip over a card and think of a sentence using the word on the card. Ask him to record the sentence into the tape recorder. Pass the recorder to the next person and repeat.

❹ When all the cards have been used and all the sentences recorded, rewind the tape and play back the story you've all created! (If you don't have a tape recorder, write the sentences on paper and pass it around, then have one person read the entire story at the end.) If the story is really good, put it into a book or act it out on video!

26 WHO'S THE DUMMY?

Here's one activity where it's OK for you to put words into someone else's mouth.

WHAT YOU'LL NEED
• **a puppet**

DIRECTIONS

❶ First, practice. Sit or stand in front of a mirror and watch your mouth move as you say the following sentence slowly: "She sells seashells by the seashore." Then try to say it with your teeth clenched and your lips slightly parted. Repeat until you can say the sentence without moving your lips.

❷ Now try saying the alphabet. You will have trouble with the letters that require you to put your lips together. Try substituting the following sounds: instead of B, say D; instead of F, say S; instead of M, say N; instead of P, say T; instead of V, say "thee"; instead of W, say "duddle-you"; instead of Y, say I.

❸ After you've practiced enough, pick up the puppet and try talking with it. Tell knock-knock jokes, poems, and riddles. Remember to open and close the puppet's mouth whenever the puppet is speaking (while keeping your own mouth closed or in a smile), and open and close your own when you are supposed to be talking. When you're ready to perform, gather family and friends and put on a show!

S U R F ' S
U P

Who says TV is just for passive couch potatoes? Here's a game that will keep you—and your friends—on your toes.

WHAT YOU'LL NEED
• two to five people • paper • pen or pencil
• television with remote control • clock or watch with a second hand

DIRECTIONS

❶ With your friends, write down a list of 10 things you see often on television. For example: potato chips, coffee mug, khaki pants, baby, trash can, pizza, lamp, gym shoe, table, basketball.

❷ Choose one person to operate the remote. That person begins channel-surfing, staying on each channel for 5 to 10 seconds (or whatever amount of time you and your friends decide on).

❸ The first person to identify an item on the list calls out "Surf's up!" and names the item. That person gets a point. In a tie, both people get a point. When all 10 things have been identified, tally up the points to find out who the Super Surfer is.

SURF'S UP! ~ COFFEE MUG.

One Cup HOT

❹ Pass the remote to the next person and play again, making up a new list.

28

SNOWLESS SNOWMAN

Why wait for winter to make a snowman when you can make one right in your own kitchen?

WHAT YOU'LL NEED
- about 1 cup soap flakes • mixing bowl • toothpicks
- snowman decorations (buttons, yarn, twigs, etc.)

DIRECTIONS

1 Put a cupful (it does not have to be exact) of soap flakes into the bowl.

2 Add hot tap water a little at a time and stir with a spoon. Keep adding water until the mixture looks and feels like clay.

3 Mold your soap clay into a snowman or other fun snow creature. If you're making a snowman, you may want to insert a toothpick or two through the middle of the center ball as shown to hold it together.

4 Decorate your snowy friend and give it a name!

Chilly
the
Snowman

38

FRUITY FUN

These two fruity drinks are sure to keep you refreshed on a warm spring, summer, or fall afternoon. They're great in the winter, too!

JUICE CUPS

WHAT YOU'LL NEED
• any flavored fruit juice • small paper cup

DIRECTIONS

❶ Fill the paper cup two-thirds full with juice.

❷ Carefully place the cup in the freezer.

❸ After half an hour, the juice will be slushy. If you wait too long, it will be frozen solid.

❹ Use a spoon to scoop the fruity slush out of the cup. Enjoy!

FRUIT SMOOTHIE

WHAT YOU'LL NEED
• blender • I cup low-fat vanilla yogurt
• I cup ice • I cup orange juice
• any of the following: bananas, strawberries, blueberries, oranges, peaches, pineapple, raspberries, or other fruit

DIRECTIONS

❶ In a blender, combine the yogurt, ice, and juice until smooth.

❷ Blend in your choice of fruit and pour the smoothie into a glass.

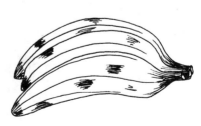

SUNNY-DAY
UMBRELLA

Ever heard the saying "Let a smile be your umbrella"? But in a heavy downpour, that's easier said than done! Once you finish this craft, you can carry sunshine wherever you go.

WHAT YOU'LL NEED

• **newspapers** • **smock or old shirt** • **plain, light blue (or other light color) umbrella**
• **waterproof slick paint pens (white, red, yellow, dark blue)** • **three sponges**

DIRECTIONS

❶ Spread newspapers over your work area and put on the smock. Open the umbrella and lay it on the newspapers. Don't worry, it won't bring bad luck!

❷ First, make the ocean. Squeeze a few overlapping lines of blue and white paint about 2 inches from the bottom edge of the umbrella. Holding the umbrella in one hand and the first sponge in the other, wipe the sponge lightly across the paint, using small strokes to create an ocean around the bottom of the umbrella.

❸ Cut the second sponge into a triangle and the third into a cloud shape. Squeeze red paint onto the triangle sponge and spread the paint evenly using a scrap piece of sponge.

❹ Now make a sailboat. Holding the umbrella in one hand, press the triangle sponge onto the umbrella five times close together to create the body of the boat as shown. Then press the triangle twice above the boat to create the sails. Connect the sails and body of your boat with the red paint pen.

40

5 Spread white paint on the cloud-shaped sponge and spread it evenly using a scrap piece of sponge. Press the shape around the top of the umbrella to create a cloudy sky.

6 For the sun, squeeze a circle of yellow paint and smooth it out with a sponge scrap. Add yellow and white rays coming out of the sun. Let the umbrella dry completely before closing it.

A WHAT?

If you think you don't get confused easily, just wait until you play this game. It's enough to drive anyone batty!

WHAT YOU'LL NEED

• five or more people • lots of small objects with one-syllable names
(such as a ball, a key, and a pen), at least one for each person playing

DIRECTIONS

❶ Have the players sit in a circle. Select a leader. Pile all of the objects to the left of the leader. The leader picks up one object and hands it to the person to her left, saying, for example, "This is a ball."

❷ The person to the leader's left takes the object and asks, "A what?" The leader replies, "A ball." The person asks again, "A what?" and the leader repeats, "A ball." The person then says, "Oh! A ball."

❸ Doesn't sound very confusing, does it? Just wait. The leader then picks up a second object and again hands it to the person on her left, saying, for example, "This is a key," and the same conversation takes place.

❹ Here's where the confusion begins. *At the same time that the leader picks up the second object,* the person holding the first object must turn to the person on her left and start the same conversation she just had with the leader, beginning with "This is a ball." Then she must turn back to the leader and say "A what?" in response to the key. In other words, each player will be carrying on two conversations at once.

❺ The conversation continues around the circle. When the first object reaches the last person in the circle, she exchanges a conversation with the leader, and then the leader places the object back into the pile. See how many items you can pass around without messing up or bursting into giggles!

P U Z Z L E
F R A M E

The next time you're thinking of tossing out a puzzle that has missing pieces, why not turn it into a great gift?

WHAT YOU'LL NEED

• **heavy cardboard (a brown corrugated box works best)** • **pencil** • **3-by-5-inch index card**
• **rubber cement** • **photo** • **jigsaw puzzle with missing pieces**

DIRECTIONS

1 Measure a 5-by-7-inch rectangle on the cardboard and mark it off with the pencil. Cut out the rectangle. Using the rectangle as a template, cut out another rectangle of the same size.

2 Center the index card on the first rectangle and mark it off. Cut out the shape. (It's OK if you need to make a cut into the outer rectangle in order to get to the inner one. The cut will be covered by puzzle pieces.)

3 Lay the outer rectangle on top of the second rectangle. Place the index card inside the hole and hold it there. With your other hand, lift up the outer rectangle as shown and put it aside.

4 Trace around the index card exactly where it is as shown. Remove the card.

5 Use rubber cement to attach puzzle pieces to the outer rectangle. The pieces should overlap each other and hang slightly over the opening in the center. This will be your outer frame.

6 Glue the outer frame to the second rectangle on three sides: left, right, and bottom. Leave the top unglued so that you can slide the photo in.

7 Measure a 1-by-5-inch rectangle on a cardboard scrap and cut it out. Bend the rectangle 1 inch from the end and apply rubber cement on the 1-inch area. Attach this part to the back middle of your frame to create a stand.

8 Slip in a favorite photo of you and a friend and give it as a gift. Write a card to go with it that says, "My puzzle pieces are missing and you've been framed!"

CARTOON

....

MADNESS

Get goofy when you play this cartoon captioning game.

WHAT YOU'LL NEED
• four or more people • a few weeks' worth of Sunday funnies
• white correction fluid • felt-tip pens, any color

DIRECTIONS

1 Cut out four comic strips per person and white-out the words in the captions or dialogue bubbles.

2 Sit in a circle and place the comics in the center. Hold up the comics one by one. As a group or individually, come up with your own captions or dialogue. Write them in with a felt-tip pen. Draw any missing elements into the scene, too, if you wish.

3 When you're finished, lay out all the comics in the center and choose your favorites.

FINGER FOLLIES

There are finger puppets, and there are finger puppets, but these are made from real fingers!

WHAT YOU'LL NEED

• felt • white glue • sequins • cotton balls • ribbons • water-based felt-tip pens

DIRECTIONS

❶ Wash and dry your hands well. Pick a hand to decorate. It's best to decorate the hand you don't write with.

❷ You'll be working on one finger at a time. First, cut a piece of felt to fit around one finger. Then wrap it around a finger just below the top knuckle, and secure it with glue. Do not glue the felt to your finger. Accessorize by gluing on sequins to create a bowtie or a row of buttons.

❸ Pull apart a cotton ball and sculpt it into a hairstyle. Fit it over the tip of your finger like a helmet. Now remove it and spread a little glue on the area that will cover your fingertip. Set it aside to dry and harden. Glue on sequins, ribbon, or felt to create a hat or hair accessories. Draw eyes and a mouth on your finger, and put the cotton hair back on.

❹ Repeat for the rest of the fingers on that hand. Once your puppets are decked out in their finest, gather an audience and put on a show!

STAR

QUALITY

Ham it up with your friends and catch it on tape.

WHAT YOU'LL NEED
• three or more friends • video camera

DIRECTIONS

❶ With your friends, brainstorm what kind of movie you want to make. It can be a documentary in which you film your everyday activities, or it can be a movie with characters, props, a story line, and a script. If you are doing a documentary, pick a subject and decide what you want to focus on.

❷ Select one person to be the first camera operator, but switch off so that everyone gets a chance to be in the film and work the camera. Before you start filming, decide who will direct, who will write the script and dialogue, who will act in the film, who will be in charge of costumes and props, and any other duties you can think of.

❸ When you're ready to roll, set up the camera, props, and other equipment, put the actors in position, and start shooting!

DELICIOUS DIRT

Make this delicious treat to enjoy after dinner—and after you've finished your homework. Mud never tasted so good!

WHAT YOU'LL NEED
• four chocolate pudding cups • four clear plastic cups
• six chocolate cookies (such as Oreos) • resealable plastic bag
• rolling pin • 12 gummy worms

DIRECTIONS

1 Spoon the contents of each pudding cup into a plastic cup.

2 Place the cookies in the resealable bag. Squeeze out as much air as you can and seal it. Run the rolling pin over the bag to crush the cookies into crumbs as shown.

I CAN'T BELIEVE IT'S NOT DIRT!

3 Sprinkle the crumbs over the top of the pudding in each cup.

4 Insert three gummy worms through the crumb layer and into the pudding in each cup.

ON WITH
THE SHOW

Dazzle your family and friends with this easy-to-make television screen that showcases your drawing and storytelling talents.

WHAT YOU'LL NEED

• **Lucite (clear acrylic resin) magnetic photo frame**
• **sheet of cardboard, about 3 inches larger than the frame on all sides**
• **acrylic paints and paintbrush** • **two bottle caps**
• **roll of butcher paper, same width as the Lucite frame**
• **colored pencils, markers, or crayons** • **glue**

DIRECTIONS

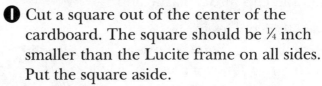

❶ Cut a square out of the center of the cardboard. The square should be ¼ inch smaller than the Lucite frame on all sides. Put the square aside.

❷ Cut the remaining cardboard "frame" into the shape of an old-fashioned TV as shown. The TV should extend 3 inches past each side of the Lucite frame. Paint your TV and let dry. Paint the two bottle caps black and let dry.

❸ Now create your filmstrip. Measure the height of the Lucite frame. Mark off the roll of paper to create frames the same size as the Lucite frame. Leave 6 extra inches at the top.

❹ Think of a story and illustrate each frame of the filmstrip to tell your story. You can write dialogue bubbles, or you and a friend can write a script to act out as you unroll the cartoon. Draw the pictures in order from top to bottom so that the story will play itself out as you pull the strip up. Leave the 6 inches at the top blank. After the last frame, cut your filmstrip off the roll.

❺ Glue the cardboard TV to the Lucite frame. Then glue on the two bottle caps for the control knobs. Thread your filmstrip through the bottom of the frame and position it so that the first picture is in the TV window. Pull the filmstrip through the frame from the top, stopping at each frame. Create a whole film library!

SUNSET
BEACH

Create a beautiful landscape painting—without paints!

WHAT YOU'LL NEED
• newspapers • heavy-stock white watercolor paper
• water-based felt-tip markers • paintbrush • paper towels

DIRECTIONS

❶ Spread newspapers to protect your workspace.

❷ Create a beach landscape on the watercolor paper using the markers. For the sky, use sunset colors. Don't blend the colors together—that will happen automatically in the next step.

❸ Dip the paintbrush in water, then dab at the colors on the paper. They should start to blend like watercolors. If the colors get too runny, lay a paper towel lightly on top to blot the excess water, but don't press down on it. Lift up the towel and continue "painting."

❹ Once you're finished with your landscape, set it aside to dry. When people ask how you made such a beautiful picture, tell them you used water. That will leave them scratching their heads!

PERFECT PETS

You probably have so many things to do each day that you couldn't possibly take on one more task. But the only maintenance these little critters require is fresh water every few weeks. Think you can manage that? Sure you can!

WHAT YOU'LL NEED

- **empty foam trays (such as meat trays, takeout-food cartons, egg cartons)**
- **waterproof markers • fishing line**
- **waterproof bonding glue**
- **bag or box of small seashells**
- **fishbowl**

DIRECTIONS

❶ Cut the trays into three or four different fish shapes and color them with the markers. Cut one piece of fishing line for each fish. Vary the lengths, starting with 2 or 3 inches.

❷ Glue the bottom of each fish to one end of each fishing line. Glue the other end of each line to a seashell. Let dry.

❸ Fill the bottom of the fishbowl with a ½-inch layer of seashells. Place the fish into the fishbowl, then fill with water.

❹ The fish should float and bob in the water. If they are lying on top of the water, don't worry— they're not dead! Just take them out and shorten the fishing line.

SENTENCE

SCRABBLE

Do you have a way with words? Play this game alone or challenge your friends. In this game, creativity is everything, and no sentence is too silly.

WHAT YOU'LL NEED
• **one to five players** • **50 index cards** • **pen or pencil** • **paper to keep score**

DIRECTIONS

1 Prepare by following steps 1 through 3. Separate the index cards into five stacks of 10 cards each. On the first stack, write a noun on each card. (A noun is a person, place, or thing, such as *dog, boy, school, friend, the president.*) On the second stack, write a verb on each card. (A verb describes an action, such as *run, love, jump, eat, snore.*)

2 On the third stack, write an adjective on each. (An adjective describes a noun, such as *cold, red, stinky, happy.*) On the fourth stack, write a pronoun on each. (A pronoun replaces a noun, such as *he, me, she, us, it, them.*)

3 On the fifth stack, write these suffixes on five of the cards: *s, ly, ing, ed, ish.* On the remaining cards, write these prepositions: *of, over, between, beneath, through.*

4 Collect all the cards into one big stack and shuffle them face down. Have your friends sit in a circle and place the stack in the middle. Decide who will go first and who will keep score.

5 Have each player pick seven cards and hold them so that the other players can't see them. The first player puts down at least three cards to form a sentence. She must then draw the same number of cards that she just put down. The next player builds off one of the words from the first player's sentence to make another sentence, and the play continues around the circle. Any words that are next to each other must make a sentence. If a player cannot create a sentence, she discards one card and picks up a new one, and the next player takes a turn.

6 Each player gets one point for each word used, and 10 extra points for using all seven cards in one play.

7 When the entire stack of cards is gone, the person with the most points wins. Read all the sentences and see if you can make up a story with them!

STRING
BALLOON ART

The best part of this fun activity is the very last step—because you don't know what you're going to get!

WHAT YOU'LL NEED
• newspapers • glue • acrylic paints, various colors • paper cups
• four balloons in different shapes and sizes • ribbons, strings, and cords • glitter • pin

DIRECTIONS

❶ Spread newspapers over your work area. This will get messy!

❷ Pour ¼ cup of each color of paint into a paper cup. Mix ¼ cup glue into each cup.

❸ Blow up the balloons and tie the ends.

❹ Dip the ribbons, strings, and cords into the paint mixtures. Drape them around the balloons as shown, overlapping them as much as possible. Sprinkle with glitter for an added sparkle.

❺ When the paint is dry and the ribbons and strings are hard to the touch, pop the balloon with a pin and peel it away to reveal your three-dimensional sculpture!

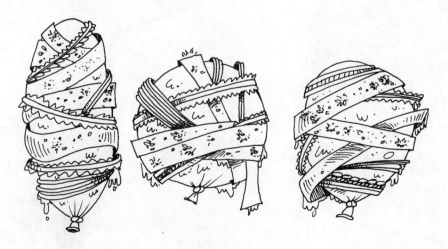

FIT TO
BE TIED

Spruce up any pair of shoes with a pair of crazy laces you design yourself.

WHAT YOU'LL NEED

• **newspapers** • **wide pair of new shoelaces** • **paint pens and slick pens**

DIRECTIONS

1 First, spread newspapers over your work area. Lay the shoelaces flat on top of the newspaper.

2 Start painting one side of the laces as shown. Make stripes, swirls, dots, wavy lines, and so on. Let dry.

3 Thread the laces through your shoes, and watch them catch people's eye as you stroll down the hall at school!

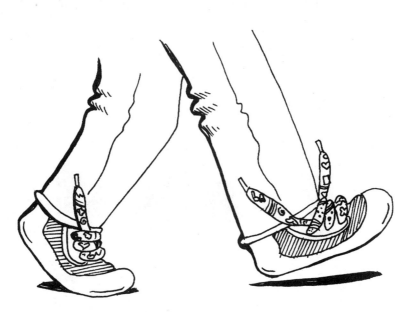

FROZEN
CHUNKY MONKEYS

You'll go ape over these chocolate-dipped bananas.

WHAT YOU'LL NEED
• four chilled bananas • four barbecue skewers • 12 ounces chocolate chips
• microwave-safe bowl • cookie sheet • wax paper
• ½ cup chopped peanuts, chopped walnuts, or candy sprinkles • small plate

DIRECTIONS

❶ Peel the bananas and pierce each one lengthwise with a skewer so that you have a banana on a stick.

❷ Pour the chocolate chips into the bowl. Microwave on high for 30 seconds. Take the bowl out of the microwave, stir, and put the bowl back into the microwave for another 30 seconds. Take the bowl out and stir again. If the chips have not yet melted, keep microwaving for 30-second intervals until they are melted.

❸ Cover the cookie sheet with wax paper. Dip each banana into the melted chocolate and swirl it around until it is covered with chocolate.

❹ Set the bananas on the wax paper and place the cookie sheet in the freezer for about 5 minutes.

❺ Pour the nuts onto the small plate. Take the cookie sheet out of the freezer. Roll each banana in the nuts as shown. Place the bananas back onto the wax paper, and put the cookie sheet back into the freezer.

❻ When the bananas are completely frozen, grab one and dig in!

SOAP
CRAYONS

Here's some good "clean" fun! Create some great graffiti in the bath or have a sprinkler party and draw on your friends with these crazy homemade crayons.

WHAT YOU'LL NEED
• **I cup soap flakes • one large and four small mixing bowls**
• **four spoons • four colors of food coloring • ice cube tray**

DIRECTIONS

1 Pour the soap flakes and 2 tablespoons hot tap water into the large mixing bowl and stir well until it becomes a thick paste. It will become difficult to stir. Get an adult's help if you wish.

2 Divide the soap among the small bowls. Add dropfuls of a different color food coloring to each and stir with a different spoon until the color is the intensity you like.

3 To make the crayons, press spoonfuls of soap into the ice cube tray. Set in a dry place for a few days to a week to harden.

4 Remove the crayons from the tray and allow them to dry for a few more days. These crayons make getting clean lots of fun!

59

WACKY
WET RELAY

On those hot summer-school days, or on any warm school day, cool off with this aquatic activity.

WHAT YOU'LL NEED
• four to eight people • pin • two paper cups • bucket of water
• two empty half-gallon containers

DIRECTIONS

❶ Poke six pinholes into the sides of each cup.

❷ Create a circular course for the race. It can be zigzag or a traditional circle. Place the bucket of water and the two containers at the starting point.

❸ Split up into two teams. Each team gets a cup and chooses a container.

❹ And they're off! The first runner on each team fills the cup with water from the bucket, balances the leaky cup on top of his head, and runs around the course. The runner can use his hand to steady the cup, but cannot hold the cup the entire time. When he gets to the end, he pours the remaining water into the container, then hands the cup to the next player. The team that fills their container first wins. Even if all the water leaks out of the cup, the runner must finish the course with the cup on his head, or else the team is disqualified.

CREATE A PRODUCT

Ever seen something advertised on TV and said to your friends, "We could come up with something better than that!" Well, here's your chance!

WHAT YOU'LL NEED
• empty box • colored markers • paper • video camera (optional)

DIRECTIONS

❶ Brainstorm a good idea for a product with your friends. It can be a spoof of an existing product or something that would fill a need in people's lives. It also should not be too difficult to make. One person acts as the scribe, writing down every idea that comes to mind. In a brainstorming session, there is no such thing as a bad idea—any idea can lead to a better one if you keep the flow of ideas moving.

❷ Once you have decided on a product and a name, break up into three teams. One group will handle marketing, another will handle packaging, and the third will create the product.

❸ The packaging group creates a logo and package using the box and markers and any other needed materials. The marketing group thinks of a slogan and writes a commercial jingle. The product group builds either a mock-up of the product or the real thing. If you are using a video camera, film your own commercial or music video to promote the product.

47 CHOCOLATE CANDY CRUNCH SURPRISE

These are sure to be a hit with chocolate lovers of all ages. See if they can guess what causes the crunch!

WHAT YOU'LL NEED

• 12 ounces semisweet or milk chocolate chips • 12 ounces butterscotch chips • two medium and one large microwave-safe bowls • large can Chun King crispy noodles • peanuts and raisins (optional) • two cookie sheets • wax paper or aluminum foil

DIRECTIONS

❶ Place half the chocolate chips into a bowl. Microwave for 1 minute and 30 seconds on high. Take the bowl out and stir, then microwave for another 30 seconds. Stir again. The chips should be starting to melt.

❷ Add the remaining chocolate chips and stir. Put the bowl back into the microwave and keep microwaving for 30-second periods—make sure to stir in between. When all the chips are melted, pour them into the large bowl.

❸ Repeat steps 1 and 2 with the butterscotch chips. Add to the melted chocolate chips and stir.

❹ Stir in the noodles a little at a time. It's OK if you break them up. Just make sure they are thoroughly covered in chocolate-butterscotch mixture so that people won't be able to see what they are.

❺ Add the peanuts and raisins (if using) and stir until everything is coated.

❻ Cover the cookie sheets with wax paper or foil. Scoop out a tablespoon of the mixture and drop it onto one sheet. Repeat, arranging the mounds in rows. Make sure they don't touch each other, or else they'll be hard to separate once they've cooled.

❼ Put the cookie sheets in the refrigerator or freezer for at least half an hour. Clean up any mess you made and put away any leftover ingredients.

❽ When the candies are hard, take them out and transfer them to a container or plate. Store them in the refrigerator or freezer until just before serving to prevent them from melting.

GEO
DUDE

Create a Chia pal with hair that really grows!

WHAT YOU'LL NEED

• two small packets grass seed • old stocking or panty hose • 2 cups sawdust
• rubber bands • glue • red felt • two googly eyes • shallow dish with rim

DIRECTIONS

1 Pour the grass seed into the stocking, then add the sawdust. (If you're using panty hose, cut the legs apart and use one leg.) Wrap the rubber band tightly around the opening to secure it. Don't stretch the stocking too much or the seeds will fall out. This is your Geo Dude's head.

2 Wrap rubber bands around sections of the sawdust-filled parts to form ears and a nose as shown. Turn the stocking upside down. Cut out a pair of lips from the red felt and glue onto the Dude's head. Glue on the googly eyes. Adjust the first rubber band so that the head has just the right shape. You may want to open up the stocking and add more sawdust if necessary. Be careful not to disturb the Dude's features.

3 Place your Dude in the bowl and add water. He'll sprout hair in a few days! Replace the water as it evaporates.

64

ODOR
EATERS

Do your gym clothes make your locker smell not-so-fresh-as-a-daisy? Looks like you need something to cure those gym-shoe blues.

WHAT YOU'LL NEED
• **poster board** • **hole puncher** • **string or twine** • **bowl** • **two cinnamon sticks**
• **dried pine needles** • **five whole cloves** • **vanilla bean** • **white glue**

DIRECTIONS

❶ Cut a shape out of the poster board, such as a sneaker, softball, soccer ball, helmet, car, or hockey stick. It should be about 4 inches long. Punch a hole in the top and tie a string through it to make a loop for hanging.

❷ Crumble the cinnamon sticks into the bowl and add the pine needles and cloves. Tear the vanilla bean into small pieces and add it to the bowl.

❸ Using an edge of scrap poster board, spread glue on one side of the shape you cut out. Sprinkle half the mixture over the glue as shown. Let set for a few minutes, then shake off the excess mixture back into the bowl. If too much goes back in, apply more glue and repeat.

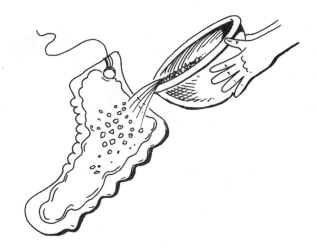

❹ Once the glue is fairly dry, turn the shape over and repeat on the other side until most of the mixture is attached to your shape.

❺ Hang your odor eater in your locker or anyplace else that needs freshening up. Any potpourri can be substituted for the cinnamon, pine, cloves, and vanilla. Make one for a friend's locker!

PAPER FLOWER BOUQUET

Whether it's "Thank you," "Happy Birthday," or "I'm sorry," if you want to "say it with flowers" but you're low on cash, a paper bouquet is the ticket.

WHAT YOU'LL NEED
• six sheets construction paper, any color • three sheets green construction paper • stapler • removable tape • wrapping paper • index card and pen

DIRECTIONS

1 First, make the flowers. Fold one of the colored sheets of construction paper into a fan pattern, then fold in half. Staple it lengthwise in the middle of the fold as shown to hold the pleats firmly in place.

2 Hold the paper at the staple end with the open end pointing up. Using scissors, round off the tip of the open end, about ¾ to 1 inch from the end as shown.

3 Now pull the sides out like a crepe paper ornament, and tape the edges together as shown. Repeat to make six flowers.

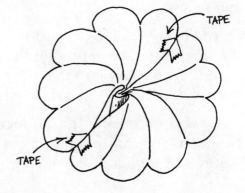

TAPE

TAPE

4 To make the stems, fold each sheet of green construction paper lengthwise and cut it in half down the center. Take each half and roll it up tightly lengthwise as shown. Tape it so that it does not unroll. Repeat until you have six stems.

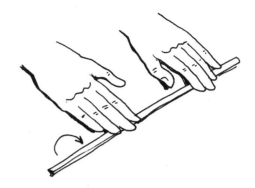

5 Now you're ready to do some flower arranging! Attach the first stem by stapling it along the back of the flower as shown. It may take three or four staples to hold it in place.

6 Gather the stems at the bottom and tape them loosely together. Wrap the wrapping paper around the stems to form a cone. Staple the tip of the cone to hold the bouquet together.

7 Fold the index card in half, write a message on the outside, and sign it on the inside. Staple it to the wrapping paper.

PARTY
LINE

No party poopers here! In this game, players try to guess each person's job by asking questions one might ask at a party.

WHAT YOU'LL NEED
• four or more people • index cards • pencil for each person
• watch or clock with a second hand

DIRECTIONS

❶ Count the number of people playing and subtract one. Give each person that number of index cards and a pencil. Have everyone write down a different job or role on each card; for example, "mom," "mail carrier," "mad scientist," and "shoe salesperson." Collect all the cards and mix them up.

❷ Select one person to be the party host. Everyone else is a guest. Have each guest pick one card and look at it. That will be her or his identity for the first round of the game. The guests should not reveal their identities to the other players.

❸ The host writes down the exact time on a blank index card, then begins asking questions to find out what each person's identity is. For example, the host can ask, "Do you work with your hands?" or "Do you wear a special uniform?" The guest must answer honestly. The guests also should pretend they are the person on the card. For example, if a boy selects a card that says "mom," he can talk in a high voice or call the host "Sweetie."

❹ The host can guess anyone's identity at any time, and can take as many guesses as needed. When the host guesses all the identities correctly, note the time on the clock and calculate how long it took.

❺ Choose another host and have each guest draw another card. Keep playing until everyone has had a chance to be host. Compare everyone's scores to see which person is the host with the most!

INDOOR
··
CAMP-OUT

Camp indoors by bringing the night sky into your very own room.

WHAT YOU'LL NEED

• one or more friends • rolls or sheets of black mural paper,
enough to cover all or part of your ceiling • packet of self-adhesive glow-in-the-dark stars
• black electrical tape • masking tape • bright table lamp • sleeping bags • flashlights

DIRECTIONS

❶ Spread the black mural paper on the floor and cover it with the stars to create the night sky. (To be really accurate, get a star map from a library or bookstore and try to re-create some of the constellations.) Attach the sheets of paper together with black electrical tape.

❷ Tear off strips of masking tape and tape them into circles, sticky side out. Stick the tape onto the back of your sky.

❸ Have an adult help you stick the sky onto the ceiling.

❹ At least an hour before the camp-out, turn on the lamp and aim it upward to give the glow-in-the-dark stars a good charge. (Or, if it has a lampshade, remove it.) Set up the sleeping bags and flashlights.

❺ When everything is set, turn off the lamp. Make sure no light is coming into the room. (Stuff a towel or blanket under the door to block out light if necessary.) Climb into the sleeping bags, gaze up at the sky, turn on your flashlights, and let the ghost stories begin!

GLOP!

This messy magic slime goes from liquid to solid and makes icky cool fun.

WHAT YOU'LL NEED
• **3 cups cornstarch • mixing bowl • food coloring (optional)**

DIRECTIONS

❶ Pour the cornstarch into the bowl. Add enough water to make a paste. Add 2 or 3 drops of food coloring if you like.

❷ Mix the paste with your hands. Add more cornstarch if the mixture gets too runny.

❸ Voilà! There's your glop! Try poking and punching it, then pick it up and let it run through your fingers. Ewwww! You've been slimed!

MEXICAN
QUESADILLA

Quesadillas (kay-suh-DEE-yuhs) are a Mexican favorite. They can be eaten for breakfast, lunch, or dinner, or as a snack or appetizer. This recipe makes one cheese quesadilla. For more gusto, try adding guacamole, chopped onions, sliced olives, or pieces of cooked chicken or beef.

WHAT YOU'LL NEED
**• one corn or flour tortilla • ¼ cup shredded cheddar or Monterey Jack cheese
• pot holders • salsa**

DIRECTIONS

❶ Place the tortilla on the plate and sprinkle the cheese over it evenly.

❷ Microwave for 35 seconds on high. Check to see if the cheese has melted. If it hasn't, rotate one-half turn and microwave for another 10 seconds on high.

❸ Remove the plate carefully using the pot holders. Put as much salsa as you like on top of the melted cheese.

❹ Fold the quesadilla in half and eat it with your hands. If it's too hot, cut it with a knife and eat it with a fork.

HOCKEY BOWLING

Combine two completely different sports and what do you get? A high-energy, fast-paced game like no other.

WHAT YOU'LL NEED
• 4 to 10 people (an even number of players) • 12 bowling pins (plastic ones are fine)
• one broom for each person • tennis ball

DIRECTIONS

1 Find a large, open paved space outdoors. Split up into two teams and mark off each team's playing field and goal. At each goal line, set up the bowling pins as you would for a game of bowling.

2 Give each player a broom. Begin by facing off over the tennis ball as you would for a hockey game. The object is to knock down all of the opposing team's pins with the tennis ball while protecting your own team's pins. If all the pins are knocked down at once, that team scores a strike (10 points). If a few pins are knocked down, keep playing until they are all knocked down. If any pins are accidentally knocked down by something other than the tennis ball, the play stops and those pins are set back up again.

3 If someone knocks down a pin on purpose using their broom or body, the opposing team takes a penalty shot. In a penalty shot, one person from the opposing team takes a free shot at the pins from half court. If the person knocks down all 10 pins or the remaining pins, his team gets a point.

4 The first team to get 10 points wins.

56 SCHOOL-YEAR SCRAPBOOK

Preserve memories of your classmates and of the past school year. It's a keepsake you'll treasure for years!

WHAT YOU'LL NEED
• **construction paper** • **hole puncher**
• **three 10-inch pieces of yarn** • **school pictures of yourself and your friends**
• **colored pens or markers** • **glue**

DIRECTIONS

❶ Cut out 10 pieces of construction paper, 7 by 10 inches each. Punch three holes along the left side (make sure the holes line up). Thread a piece of yarn through each hole and gently tie it off. Don't tie it too tightly or the pages of your album won't turn.

❷ Start the album by introducing yourself. Write "Me" at the top of the first page, then fill the rest of the page with your name, any nicknames you have, your teacher's name, your grade, and the name of your school. Glue a picture of yourself on the page.

❸ Write "Friends" at the top of the next page. Glue in pictures of your friends and write in their names. Write in the names of friends whose pictures you don't have. The "Friends" section can take up more than one page.

❹ Write "What's Hot" at the top of a new page. Fill in the names of your favorite band, your favorite movie from this year, and the latest fads at your school.

❺ Write "Cool Stuff I Do" on the next page. List all the things you do at recess or after school. Include your favorite sports and activities. Glue in either a photo or drawing of yourself playing a sport or enjoying a hobby.

6 Fill in the remaining pages with items to help you remember the school year, such as movie ticket stubs and report cards. Write about things that have happened to you or activities in which you were involved. If you're at the beginning of the school year, keep five or six pages blank so that you can add to your scrapbook as the year goes by.

7 You don't have to finish the scrapbook in one day. Once a week, take a few minutes after school to add or write in new things. Once you're all done filling the pages with happy memories, put your scrapbook in a safe place so it will keep forever!

57 PERSONALIZED PICTURE FRAME

Create your own unique picture frame to hold a special photo of you and a friend. It even makes a perfect gift for that fantastic friend!

WHAT YOU'LL NEED

• newspapers and damp washcloth • large sheet corrugated cardboard
• pen or pencil • glue that dries clear (such as Elmer's) • old magazines
• paintbrush • photo of you and a friend

DIRECTIONS

1 For messy crafts like this one, cover your work area with newspapers to make cleanup a snap. Spread newspapers on the floor also. Keep a damp washcloth nearby to catch any spilled glue and to wipe your hands while you work.

2 First, make the frame. Cut the cardboard into two squares, rectangles, or circles, both the same size. The frame should be at least 1 inch larger than your photo on all sides. (If your photo is 3 by 5 inches, then your frame needs to be 4 by 6 inches.)

3 Draw a window in the middle of one of the pieces of cardboard that is a little smaller than your photo.

4 Cut out the window. If you need to, cut into the cardboard to get to the center. That cut can be patched up later with a well-placed magazine cutout.

5 Glue the two pieces of cardboard together on three sides as shown. Leave the top open so that you can insert the photo.

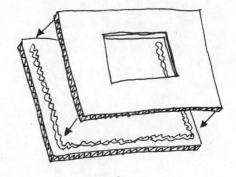

6 While the frame is drying, go through the magazines and cut out words, phrases, pictures, ads, or pieces of photos that follow a friendship theme.

❼ Organize the magazine clippings on the front of the frame. When you're satisfied with the design, spread glue evenly on the backs of the clippings with the paintbrush and attach them.

❽ Once all the clippings are glued on, paint a light, even coat of glue over the front to seal them.

❾ When everything is dry, slide in the photo. Voilà! A special, personalized picture frame!

BURST YOUR BUBBLE

Kapow! This team game is perfect if you and your friends are hankering for some loud outdoor fun!

WHAT YOU'LL NEED
• **four or more people (an even number of players)**
• **balloons in two different colors, two balloons for each person • string**

DIRECTIONS

❶ Divide into two equal teams. Each team picks one of the balloon colors and blows up the balloons in that color. Tie a piece of string to each balloon. Each team member ties one balloon to each ankle.

❷ The object of the game is to pop the other team's balloons by stomping on them with your feet. The team with the last unpopped balloon is the winner! For twice the challenge, blow up more balloons and tie two to each ankle!

❸ Before you begin, mark off the playing field to keep the game within reasonable bounds.

SCULPTURE

SNACKS

Thanks to this tasty peanut butter play dough, art never tasted so good.

WHAT YOU'LL NEED

- ½ cup smooth peanut butter • ½ cup honey
- 1 cup powdered milk • mixing bowl • paper towels
- marshmallows, chocolate chips, dried fruit, fresh fruit, and toothpicks (optional)

DIRECTIONS

❶ Wash your hands well. Put the peanut butter, honey, and powdered milk into the bowl and knead with your hands until smooth. This is your sculpting "clay."

❷ Slop some of the mixture onto a paper towel and sculpt yourself a tasty treat. If you wish, use the marshmallows, chocolate chips, fruit, and toothpicks to make your sculpture look and taste even better—but don't eat the toothpicks (duh!).

❸ If you're sculpting with friends, mix up a batch of "clay" as above for each person. Hold an art show to see whose sculpture looks the best and the yummiest!

60 SUN
CATCHERS

The best way to recycle things is to reuse them. Next time you have an empty plastic take-out container, do your part for the environment and let the sun shine in!

WHAT YOU'LL NEED
• clear plastic take-out container • water-based markers, various colors
• hole puncher • 10-inch ribbon • slick paint pens

DIRECTIONS

❶ Cut a shape out of the flat part of the take-out container, such as a butterfly, flower, star, or sun. Color it with the markers and let dry for a few minutes.

❷ Punch a hole in the top. Thread the ribbon through the hole, leaving the ends untied.

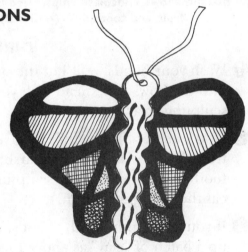

❸ Using the paint pens, draw lines between the colored areas to separate them.

❹ When your sun catcher is dry, tie the ends of the ribbon around a curtain rod so that your artwork can catch the sun shining through the window!